PICTORIAL CONNECTICUT

LAWRENCE F. WILLARD and ALVIN V. SIZER

PICTORIAL CONNECTICUT

COLLEGE AND UNIVERSITY PRESS
New Haven, Connecticut

MANUFACTURED IN THE UNITED STATES OF AMERICA BY
UNITED PRINTING SERVICES, INC.
NEW HAVEN, CONN.

Acknowledgments

The authors are grateful to Richard S. Jackson, Co-Publisher and Editor, and Lionel S. Jackson, Co-Publisher and General Manager, of the *New Haven Register* for their cooperation and kind permission to use in this book photographs which were published in the "Pictorial Connecticut" Series of the *Sunday Register Feature Magazine.*

We would also like to thank *Yankee* magazine for the use of several photographs which appeared in that publication.

THE AUTHORS

Introduction

No state in the nation has a greater capacity for absorbing the high-powered intrusions of the twentieth century without discarding all the homespun symbols of the nineteenth and the eighteenth. Now and then the protectors of the old, the scenic, and the revered have to yield to "progress," but Connecticut has fared better in preservation of weathered relics than most states lying in the path of history.

It has fared well despite its vulnerable location in the center of the industrialized Northeast, bisected by New England's busiest, broadest, and longest river, bisected again by the jugular vein connecting Manhattan and Massachusetts Bay, and crisscrossed by arteries reaching from the cities of Long Island Sound to the cities of the Hudson. For more than three centuries Connecticut has been exposed to cultural cross traffic that would have long since obliterated every vestige of the past in a less resilient commonwealth.

Through all this intrusion, Connecticut has miraculously retained the essence of Yankee character. Little factories have expanded into big factories, but the village green and the white-steepled church remain as background landmarks. Fairfield County became the bedroom for Madison Avenue, but the new residents adapted themselves to Connecticut communities rather than trying to create Riverside Drives in Greenwich, Glenbrook, or Greenfield Hill.

Throngs of vacationing escapists crowded the inland lakes and the shores of the Sound, but they did not efface the charm of either landscape or seascape. Great turnpikes and parkways angled through the hills, yet even the ugly cuts were engineered and replanted so skillfully that most of the scars soon healed. Thousands upon thousands of European nationals poured into every section of the State; they brought foreign mores and accents which were assimilated and absorbed by the implanted Yankee mores and accents.

Connecticut has grown with dignity and a difference. The old was retained along with the new. Sharp contrasts exist everywhere. Sometimes they jar, but just as often they jibe. Always—almost always—they are picturesque.

In this volume Lawrence Willard has caught the wealth of Connecticut contrasts as perhaps no New England photographer has before. Other artists have been less catholic in their choice of subject matter. Handsome photographic records of apple-blossom sentimentality, of the nostalgic, the pleasing, and the splendid in Connecticut scenery have often been made. The stark realism of the homely, the commonplace, and the prosaic has also been graphically portrayed. Mr. Willard crosses bounds. He can be closely identified with neither group. His is his own school, and the selectivity is that of the true artist. He discovers the core, wherever it may be hidden, and in this series of contrasts he has recorded the personality of Connecticut.

As free-lance and as staff photographer and feature writer for the *New Haven Register*, Mr. Willard has been pointing his camera at New England landscape and society for fifteen years. Most of the photographs in this collection have appeared in the pages of the *Register* in a weekly feature called "Pictorial Connecticut." No single regular contribution to the newspaper has stirred greater interest among subscribers. The demand for reproductions and print enlargements of the scenes has been vigorous and so continuous that he has at last been persuaded to present some of the best of them in book form.

Pictorial Connecticut will have an appeal far beyond state limits, for, as historians have often pointed out, a little of Connecticut has been transplanted in every region of the United States. Socially, intellectually and culturally, no other state in the early years of the nation exerted a wider influence.

The Connecticut heritage is widely shared, and the multitude who lay claim to it will be intensely interested in this book. Here they can see the source from which their ancestors sprang, the kind of architecture which inspired public buildings and private dwellings a thousand or five thousand miles from home, and here they will also find some hint of what has happened to the ancestral homeland.

The photographic documentation is reassuring. There is still a Connecticut Beautiful. The Yankees have kept the faith.

W. STORRS LEE

PICTORIAL CONNECTICUT

AN OPEN GATEWAY is an invitation, whether you are an actual passerby tempted to follow a road that leads—where? —or whether, as here, both your eye and your imagination are enticed, too. What might you find at the end of the road? Few of us actually travel it to find out. But we feel instinctively that whatever is there is good. So perhaps this first picture is a symbol.

It was taken on a cold winter's day in Madison, and the road leads from Route 1 to a large and very old house in the distance. But as a symbol, the road leads through the Connecticut countryside, changing, changeless. Our photographer's pictures, whether they be of towns, cities, pastures, ponds, churches, animals, boats, trees, or people will reveal many truths about Connecticut; but the essential truth is this: New values enter but old ones remain. There are swift automobiles and noisy trucks but here and there you will still find horses—though seldom pulling wagons— and many cows. Bridges and roads grow super but small ones are still in use. New buildings are taller and unadorned but there are many old ones reflecting the architecture of every period from the Colonial on. Manufacturing plants sprawl but the rural countryside is everywhere. This book, through numerous contrasting pictures, demonstrates the paradox that is Connecticut.

Fourteen

WE WON'T BE TRAVELING much on this road, although it's a superb superhighway. Despite its tremendous impact on the state's geography and economy, it appears a bit unsubstantial here in the early morning fog as it crosses the New Haven harbor. This monster emerging from the mist is the sixty-mile-an-hour, six-lane Connecticut Turnpike which opened as a toll highway in 1958 and proceeds one hundred and twenty-nine miles from the New York to the Rhode Island border, carrying both private and commercial transportation. Its side effects have not always been desirable. The Connecticut which exists outside the large industrial cities and towns is rarely seen by the through motorist—except at great speeds. "Connecticut?" said the man from the Wide Open Spaces. "Sure I been there! Went right through it on the Turnpike last summer. Didn't miss a trick!"

OUR FRIEND *did* miss this bridge and so, in fact, have many residents of the state. For you must go off the beaten track to come upon a scene like this. Our photographer discovered it in the little town of Oxford. Several years ago he set out with his camera to explore the real Connecticut—the byways and out-of-the-ways that are there for every-one who isn't in a hurry to get "somewhere else." Quite frankly, he was seeking the beautiful, not the sordid, and he found it in both nature and civilization, although his ideas of what makes beauty are distinctly his own. He also found contrasts. One of the most striking facts about Connecticut is that you can see bridges, like the one on the Turnpike in the preceding picture, which are the prototype of modern engineering and design, and yet an hour away you can find bridges like the one above with its complete absence of vehicles. Connecticut—changed but unchanging.

WHILE TOURISTS talk of the spectacular Rockies, the Grand Canyon, and Yosemite, Connecticut's quiet, unchanging beauty is closer to the hearth and the heart, so much a part of our history and our daily living that we forget to give it its due. Because Larry Willard, besides being a photographer, is also something of an artist and a poet, his pictures speak to everyone, no matter what his state or country. They bring a touch of beauty to the onlooker and a sense of pride to everyone, for just about every American is related to Connecticut in some manner or other.

Come with us, then, to visit Connecticut. The dogwood is blooming in Essex, a lovely little town on the Connecticut River, and there's a boat waiting for us should it be necessary to take to the water. (It will be, frequently.)

IN CONNECTICUT we can show you scenes of incomparable pastoral beauty. Our photographer came upon this one in the town of Deep River, in the Connecticut River Valley. A luxuriant elm, blissfully immune to the blight that is killing off its city cousins, arches out over the lily pad-studded pond. Cows graze by the water's edge. A white barn, gambrel-roofed and dormered, and silo, betoken quiet New England self-sufficiency and a reliable, prudent character. A weeping willow brushes the water's edge. Everywhere there is quiet growth. Roots go deep here—hundreds of years. In 1947 the town voted to change its name from Saybrook to Deep River. It is easy to understand why.

SOME OF CONNECTICUT's urban scenes are as famous as any in America. Here winter twilight comes to the New Haven Green where elm-framed Center Congregational Church holds the spotlight, with Yale University's Harkness Tower in the background. Anyone who knows New Haven will find this portrait evoking the warmest of associations and memories. The church is one of the country's most historic. The first services were held outdoors in 1638, and the building shown is the fourth in a sequence of religious edifices where love of God and country has been fostered by a succession of forthright clergymen. Beneath the church lies the low-ceilinged crypt where 137 of the first New Haveners, the oldest dating from 1687, lie buried. Their graves may be visited by the public. On the rear wall of the church is a tablet in memory of Theophilus Eaton, first governor of the New Haven Colony. Center is one of three famed churches on the Green, flanked by Trinity Episcopal and United Congregational.

YES, CONNECTICUT is an endless contrast of the rural and urban. Here is another example of the former, a millhouse on the bank of the Aspetuck River beside a dam in Easton. Reflection and foliage add to the charm of this millpond scene. There is an aspect to this photo worth commenting on—the "old mill" is a reconstructed one. Although a travel agent might file this away under facts not to be emphasized, we condone the fact that much of the charm of Connecticut exists because people with good taste have endeavored not only to preserve, but also to reconstruct the past.

IN CONNECTICUT the urban and the rural, the modern and the old, exist side by side. And sometimes they overlap in colorful mergers. Here a flock of rural tree swallows has usurped the urban telephone lines of Lyme. Seemingly they hold no other opinion in the world than that these utility wires were constructed for their own sedentary convenience. This picture was originally titled "Party Line." The photographer took it because he was intrigued with the possibility that the birds might be listening in on human beings conversing. And if they were, it is not difficult to surmise their reactions: "Who needs wires to talk when all you have to do is get together? Telephone communications? They're for the birds!"

IN CONNECTICUT three things are certain: death, taxes and the four seasons. It is true that other areas of the world may have seasons but because of the similarity of the weather they may exist in name only, or certain seasons may dwarf others in length or strength. In Connecticut each season is distinctly different, with a flavor and personality of its own, although equal in duration and importance. Because there is no "sameness" to the weather—remember how one of our most famous residents, Mark Twain, advised that if you didn't like the weather you had only to wait a minute? —the transience of the seasons marks off the calendar's changes emphatically and we in Connecticut are more conscious than most of time's passage. In spring the dogwood flowers in glory and is found both wild and transplanted. In this picture it grows in its natural habitat on a slope in Northford overlooking fertile farmlands in the Connecticut Valley basin. The dogwood is followed by the emergence of the state flower, the mountain laurel.

WHEN WE WERE A BOY and suffering from some real or imagined slight from family or friends, we used to wander off into a nearby daisy field, lie on our back, chew a piece of grass, and gaze up at New England clouds. Growing up brought the realization that the psychiatrist offered the same service for twenty-five dollars a session and up. Here is such a daisy field, with lone big tree, smaller trees and bushes and New England clouds, all on a summer's day in Farmington. If ever—mind you, we said "ever"—there comes a letdown in Connecticut Yankee "git up and go," it comes in summer on a day like this, in a place like this, when it seems that lying down in such a field might be the answer to all your problems.

AUTUMN BRINGS A RETURN of responsibilities to the Nutmegger. Back to work, back to school, and back to raking leaves —for the leaves are relentless every fall. For the burgeoning beauty of their birth in spring, their lush maturity in summer, and their glorious senescence in September and October, they exact the payment of this November ritual in Whitneyville, a section of Hamden. This is the last lap of the leaf-raking task; the limbs are almost bare and on one branch, if you look closely, you can see a bird's nest, exposed now that camouflage and protection are no longer needed.

WINTER IN CONNECTICUT is not for the fainthearted. Nor for the lazy. Nor for the unimaginative. It can be nasty—and it can be beautiful. It is for the young in body, or in heart, whose blood still sings in the veins. Nature exacts a heavy toll in hardship, sickness, and just plain discomfort. And in these days of mobile living Winter is the bane of the motorist. It offers just one compensation—but it is a matchless and imposing one—scenes of magic and art beyond duplication. Here winter has descended upon a fountain in Chase Park in Waterbury and while it has not succeeded—as yet—in stopping the flow, it is freezing the water almost as soon as it falls.

WINTER DOES NOT DISCRIMINATE in Connecticut. It bestows its offerings on all alike, city and town, suburban split-level and downtown apartment house. It makes one recompense for its relentless, inescapable assault—it beautifies whatever it touches, whether it be coal pile or brook, slum dwelling or farm. Its artistry is spoiled only by man. In this scene, photographed along Peck Hill Road in Woodbridge, man has not appeared except through the unobtrusive medium of the photographer. Nothing mars the perfection of the newly fallen snow as the late afternoon sun sends shadows streaking among the birches to form a pattern of horizontal and vertical lines.

THESE RATHER DRAB and old-fashioned red brick apartments along New Haven's Orange Street have been incomparably enhanced by the first snowfall of winter. Such pictures must be made quickly, in sad realization that in the city they must be filmed before man and the sun join forces to destroy their subjects. The first few footprints can add something to a picture; beyond that point beauty begins to vanish.

MEANWHILE, BACK IN THE COUNTRY, a rippling stream winds its way through barren trees in snow-covered Connecticut woodlands, creating this picturesque landscape at Wahocastinook Creek—or Fell Kill—in the center of Salisbury. The brook fights to maintain its artery against the encroaching overhang of snow and ice. Mottled sycamores fill the forest. The silence is complete except for the gurgle of water. Winter has achieved a portrait in black and white. "I didn't paint it," said the cameraman. "I just photographed the painting."

WINTER IS A MIRACLE WORKER. It can transform the commonplace into the unusual, replace the aspect of other seasons with its own brand of charm, and turn the prosaic into the unexpected. Here it has moved into a cornfield that flourished in the summer and was harvested in the fall and, without concealing it completely, has added its own distinctive touches. The result is a scene where sun and snow and cornstalk have cooperated in the production of winter loveliness, which the photographer discovered and recorded in the town of Chester, near the Connecticut River.

NOW WINTER PASSES and summer finds water transportation freed from icy grasp and mobile again. What are we waiting for, folks? We've got the boats and the oars and the pond (Deer Lake in Killingworth). If you'll just move these oars a bit—we're not about to break any speed records—we might see some fish jump and find a pond lily or two, or an old turtle sunning himself on a rotting log. This scene is typical of hundreds in the state where there are small mooring places, rowboats of varying vintage and description, and a thousand interesting things to see.

WHEN YOU START TALKING about boats you immediately find yourself talking about boys. The connection is not merely alliterative—they just seem to go together. You remember what Kenneth Grahame wrote in *The Wind in the Willows*: "There is nothing—absolutely nothing—half so much worth doing as simply messing about in boats . . . or with boats . . . in or out of 'em, it doesn't matter." Boats are one of the reasons—take it from one who knows—why it's wonderful to be a boy in Connecticut. The possibilities for adventure and dreaming are endless. And things haven't changed too much through the years except that there are fewer chores nowadays and more time for fun. Of course, there's still school. But in summer there's not even that. You can go exploring and find yourself the hulk of a rotting boat, as these boys have, on the Thames River near Gales Ferry, climb up on it at low tide, and talk about fixing it up and heading out to sea. After all, it isn't in such bad shape, really. A few boards . . . a few nails . . . and——

"A BOY'S WILL is the wind's will and the thoughts of youth are long, long thoughts," observed Henry Wadsworth Longfellow. There are always time and place in Connecticut for boys to indulge in less strenuous activities than scrambling on boats—daydreaming, for instance. There is always a fine view from Connecticut hilltops. And who knows what you might see? These boys, for example, are looking across the Thames River toward New London, perhaps to catch a glimpse of a nuclear submarine en route to the Naval Base. The mere possibility is enough to start a lad dreaming of a million things he might be when he grows up. Atomic scientist, submarine commander, admiral, maybe even presi——

THIS LAD could have a big blue on his hook and be none the wiser. You can just read his thoughts as his attention wanders from salt water fishing off the mouth of the Connecticut River at Old Saybrook—"Those lucky kids on that boat! Man, someday I'm going to have me one of those!" Don't waste time feeling sorry for him. Chances are good he'll grow up to achieve his wish—per capita income in Connecticut exceeds that of any other state in the Union.

SOMETIMES THE POSSIBILITIES for boys in Connecticut are not apparent to blasé grownups. They require exercise of the imagination. For example, to an adult this will be merely a handsome winter picture of the Mad River, which has been known to go on destructive rampages in Winsted. The onlooker will note that the reflection of the sun, peeking through the clouds, gives the rippling waters an even brighter appearance than the melting snow along the river's edge. But the boy will have a different slant on the scene. What a swell chance to make your way out on one of the rocks and see how far down the river you can go jumping from boulder to boulder! Of course, you may get a little wet. And Mom may get a little mad! But, nothing ventured, nothing gained.

AGAIN, IS THIS just an unusual arch of fallen trees across Mill River in South Meriden? Not to the boy looking for adventure. Soon one will come along, survey the situation, and his eyes will light up. Now if I were to shinny out along one of these trees, I could make my way down the other tree and I'd be over on the other side of the stream without getting wet (maybe).

Some say nature is impersonal. Don't believe it for a moment. Who do you think created situations like this for youth, in pitying awareness of Wordsworth's warning that "Shades of the prison-house begin to close upon the growing boy"?

SOME OF THE POSSIBILITIES nature has created for boys haven't changed for many generations in Connecticut. While it's true that some modern lads may have fiberglass or stainless steel swimming pools in their back yards, others frequent the ol' swimmin' hole just as Dad and Granddad did. You'll find this shaded pool in Woodbury under an iron bridge crossing the Pomperaug. The kids have added some wooden cleats and a long rope so that they can swing off into the cool water. Looks like more fun than we've had in a long time.

WHEN A BOY GROWS UP and the opposite sex charms her way into his recreation plans, he finds that Connecticut still offers infinite possibilities. And so does the water! But since the days of the ol' swimmin' hole some new wrinkles have been added. Boy meets girl and both water ski off into the sunset. The new aquatic sport has taken a firm hold and has proven a popular attraction for adolescents and young adults. Here a couple have set out from the dock on the Thames River below Norwich and are having themselves some real fun.

EVER NOTICE SOMETHING about young lovers? Even in a crowd they can usually manage to get away by themselves. And if they can't, it doesn't matter. They can be oblivious to the world. Romance generally finds an opportunity to bloom in Connecticut. Despite the people who get in the way in a popular recreation spot, like Beardsley Park in Bridgeport, it is usually possible to withdraw a bit "from the madding crowd" for a bit of heart to heart, as this couple have done. A picnic lunch, a nice summer's day, an idyllic setting, and a compatible twosome. From this sort of situation a courtship can get off to a winging start.

HERE BOY AND GIRL share an exciting sport—fishing in the Salmon River at East Haddam. While onlookers observe from the shore, this pair have waded out in search of trout. Perhaps they won't catch a thing, but the memory of this glorious day and the recollection of an experience shared in the bracing fresh air and water of Connecticut may have given them something to treasure and seek to repeat often during a lifetime.

EVEN IN WINTER the water does not forsake boy and girl in search of activities to share. It provides for skating, skiing, sliding, and an even more unusual sport—iceboating. When frigid winds blow each year, iceboat enthusiasts head for Bantam Lake, covering 900 acres southwest of Litchfield at an elevation of 896 feet. The "boaters" whiz around at an exhilarating speed. They stage races and have a peppy, invigorating time. They also have memories which are a switch on the usual routine. They can say, "Remember the fun we had last winter?"

IF YOU WERE A BOY with a girl, or a girl with a boy, how would you like to stroll down this country lane in Orange in Maytime with the apple trees in bloom and no obstacles on the road ahead? The rail fence has seen better days and maybe someday someone will fix it. And maybe not. If Jeannette MacDonald and Nelson Eddy were to come sauntering down this road hand-in-hand singing, "Sweetheart, Sweetheart, Sweetheart," it wouldn't surprise us a mite. But before you label the scene old-fashioned, look carefully and you'll see tire treads in the dirt. For this, again, is the paradox of Connecticut—things change, but they are unchanging. This isn't the time for philosophy, however. Take your girl by the hand and set forth into a promising future.

IF YOU CORRESPOND with your girl these days you don't leave your billet-doux in the hollow trunk of an apple tree. Here is where it's more likely to be found, for something has been added to those old-fashioned boy-walks-girl country lanes these days. The road still looks about country-size and not too heavily patronized by cars, but the rural mail-boxes (we count about twenty-five) testify that there are suburbanites in residence somewhere near. They signify that progress in the form of the motorized mailman has not reached all the byways and countryside roads as yet and those desirous of receiving mail must cluster their receptacles on the nearby "main highway" as this group in Shelton has done.

AS THE YOUNG PEOPLE grow up and seek advanced schooling they don't have to go far from home. Connecticut has been singularly blessed in the field of secondary and college education. Despite its small size, the state has an abundance of good preparatory schools, high schools, and private and public colleges and universities. The most famous of them all, Yale University in New Haven, is most often depicted by much-photographed Harkness Tower, shown here. The gothic structure is 221 feet high and on the walls of the room at its base are wood carvings illustrating the history of this, the country's third oldest college. Founded in 1701, Ivy League Yale has always led in the fight for the fundamental rights of man. Yale's motto, "Lux et Veritas"— Light and Truth—celebrates two virtues freedom espouses, and the rallying cry, "For God, for Country, and for Yale," is not necessarily an anticlimax, as Harvard men would have you believe, but three bulwarks of liberty.

CONNECTICUT'S PARADOX of the old and new existing side by side is demonstrated in surprising fashion by this picture. What you are actually looking at is part of the University of Connecticut, including the dairy, at Storrs. This is the fastest growing university in the state and largest in number of undergraduates. And yet it can be photographed with a pastoral touch. State-supported college education has expanded greatly in recent years in an energetic attempt to keep pace with the surge in demand for entrance. There is a network of four state colleges, formerly called teachers' colleges, and before that, normal schools. UCONN started out in 1881 as Storrs Agricultural College and now has a roster of about 10,000 students and faculty. Its student body has increased tenfold since only 1935. The growth of no institution in the state has been more amazing than UCONN's. Although it can be charmingly photographed, no one would dare to call the University of Connecticut a "cow college" any more.

AS THE NEW COMES IN, a determined effort is made to keep strong the links with what is worthwhile in the past. There is proof of that in this photograph of a dormitory at Fairfield University, Gonzaga Hall, constructed in the post-World War II era but displaying a Gregorian chant in bricks implanted on one wall. Fairfield was founded by the Jesuits in 1942 and now has over 1,300 students. Its steady expansion has been typical of the amazing growth of the state's educational institutions in our time. The older, established colleges such as Yale (1701), Trinity (1823), Wesleyan (1831), University of Connecticut (1881), and Connecticut College for Women (1911), have not been able to keep up with the increased demand for education that has arisen since the first quarter of this century. As a consequence, an entirely new group of colleges like Fairfield has come into being, including the Universities of Bridgeport and Hartford, New Haven College, Quinnipiac College, Albertus Magnus and Annhurst.

WHEN IT COMES to private preparatory schools, few states are in the same league with Connecticut. The roster is impressive, ranging all the way from Hopkins Grammar School, 1660, which predates Yale University by more than four decades, to post-World War II schools like Fairfield Prep. Among the other outstanding ones are Cheshire Academy, Suffield Academy, Miss Porter's, Gunnery, Westminster, Taft, Hotchkiss, Pomfret, Salisbury, Loomis, Kent, Westover, Canterbury, South Kent, Wooster and Avon Old Farms. The largest and one of the country's top private schools is Choate, at Wallingford, founded in 1896 by Judge William G. Choate. Choate's superb physical plant is represented here by a photograph of its infirmary which has the status of a hospital and is, in fact, named Archbold Hospital.

INSTITUTIONS OF HIGHER LEARNING have always been strong-holds of freedom, symbolizing the concepts of independence of thought and character which are its components. Freedom can also be symbolized in the grandeur of the State Capitol, an imposing structure of marble and granite overlooking Hartford's Bushnell Park. Topped by a gleaming gold dome, the State House was opened in January 1879. Its construction cost $2,532,524. Important personalities and events in the state's history are commemorated both within and without the building in the form of statues, paintings, historic relics, and other adornments. Here you will find the tombstone of that resourceful patriot, General Israel Putnam, who ordered, "Don't fire until you see the whites of their eyes!" Connecticut has always been known for its sturdy sense of independence and self-reliance. Its nicknames are "The Land of Steady Habits" and "The Constitution State," the latter because this state had the first written constitution of any known government on this continent; the Constitution of the United States was largely based upon it. Small wonder you think of Connecticut when you think of freedom.

BUT FREEDOM in Connecticut doesn't have to be illustrated by the grandeur of the State Capitol in Hartford or a lofty tower at Yale University. It is also this, and probably essentially and basically this: the common man, who is concerned with the very soil of Connecticut. On a farm near Kent (there are still 8,292 in the state at last count) a ninety-five-year-old farmer ties up the corn and puts it in shocks as he has always done and as it has always been done. Only the gleam of the utility wires along the road places this scene in the twentieth century. Resourceful, independent, hard-working, this is a free man in a free state. He gives you an idea of what freedom means. The next series of pictures offers some other ideas.

WHY GET HIGHFALUTIN about it? This is freedom! Everything about this picture tells you what it means to be free. The photographer took this action picture of two palomino horses in a woodland pasture off Bethany Mountain Road in Cheshire. It's one of his favorite shots, and ours too. Freedom means being unfettered, unsaddled, frisky, full of zip, able to go places so long as you don't abuse other people's rights. In Connecticut if you want to, you have the right to— —(turn page)

——take a chance!
(This white cat was snapped jumping from one window
ledge to another at an apartment building in New Haven.)

YOU ALSO HAVE THE RIGHT to bring up your children in a pleasant, healthful surrounding, with no one to bother you if you behave.

(This pastoral scene may look like typical English countryside but it's Connecticut—at Durham.)

YOU HAVE THE RIGHT to pick your own friends and to assemble peaceably with them.

(Taken off Tuttle Avenue in Hamden. There are some 4,000 horses and mules in Connecticut.)

FREEDOM GIVES YOU THE RIGHT to share municipal facilities despite your differences in physical appearance or color. And the right to mind your own business and be left alone.

(The pigeons and the people who share the New Haven Green have been living lives of mutual respect for a long time now.)

ALSO IMPORTANT is the right to live in dignity and peace and with no unwarranted invasion of privacy.

(This pair of swans was photographed in the early morning fog at Hubbard Park, Meriden.)

WHEN ALL IS SAID AND DONE, freedom is the simple right to put your face to the sun and look your best. And the right to a little of the good earth to accomplish it.

(This field of Queen Anne's lace was photographed in Orange. Mother Nature has the greenest thumb of all. She does no plowing, raking, or weeding. Yet her results are in evidence in fields and woodlands throughout Connecticut.)

AND WHEN YOUR DAYS OF TOIL are over, freedom gives you the right to seek out a quiet pasture, enjoy the fruits of a life well spent, and relax in contemplation.

(This portrait of clouds, trees, and horses came from Southbury.)

WE WOULD LIKE TO THINK scenes of freedom in Connecticut are timeless—have always been here, will always be here. We know better. Their preservation demands "eternal vigilance." But there *are* timeless scenes in the state, some of which we show you in these next few pictures. For example, look at this swampland near the Wallingford-Durham line and reflect on these facts: An average of 517.5 persons per square mile lives in Connecticut, the fourth most densely populated state in the Union. There are only two states smaller in size than Connecticut, which has 169 cities and towns and 5,261 manufacturing establishments. And yet Connecticut has many scenes, like this one, which are virtually timeless. Try to date this photograph. You will be stumped unless you cheat on us and point out that it must have been taken since the invention of the camera!

WILD FERNS GROW in a Connecticut forest at Easton the same way they have always grown, time out of mind. Long before the Indians came they were creating the same translucent, cross-thatched pattern of green intricacy, defying any hope of man to duplicate it. They even recall descriptions of the lush foliage of prehistoric times as they display their beauty, probably long unappreciated until the photographer happened along. They couldn't care less. Beauty is its own excuse for being. And beauty, like so much of the state they embellish, is timeless.

THIS PHOTOGRAPH of the Quinnipiac River in Wallingford is not merely timeless, it is "other worldly." Not only are man and animal absent; one feels they do not even belong. Winter has cloaked the Quinnipiac with magic and imbued it with a ghostly, mystic aura. One is almost ready to swear that man's presence has never been felt here and that it will be an eon or two before he appears on the scene. And yet, because, as we have said, Connecticut is a paradox, one must point out that the same Quinnipiac is elsewhere lined with factories and too dirty to swim in, although an antipollution campaign is being conducted to remedy this.

IN THE FOREGROUND, waiting for a chance to shoot a duck, a hidden Indian may lie waiting—or is it a Colonial settler, a Civil War returnee, or a motorist who stopped only yesterday with his camera? Perhaps we cannot say that this photograph is timeless, since bird life dates it as in the age of vertebrates, but it defies any closer dating. For despite its reputation as a thickly populated industrial state, much of Connecticut remains as it has always been—picturesque, idyllic, seemingly eternal. This photograph of morning haze on Community Lake in Wallingford illustrates the unchanging aspect of some of Connecticut's scenery as seagulls venture inland from the littoral in search of breakfast.

THOUGH NATURE be timeless and man mortal, they have one thing in common—each imposes patterns on our world. Nature's patterns are seemingly artless and unstudied, but the result is art. The photographer has only to seek, recognize, and record. Here in this landscape of a swamp at Shelton, Nature's pattern consists mostly of perpendicular lines of cat-o'-nine tails and trees reaching skyward. Her systems just grew this way, and the imperfection of occasionally slanting or curving lines only adds the stamp of perfection to her work of art.

MAN'S PATTERN is no less artistic, as shown in the main complex of the New Haven Railroad in New Haven, but there is a difference. There is no artless art here. Every line, represented by wires and tracks, is going somewhere definite. These many rails and girders and wires exist because they are all needed. Each has a purpose and the slanting wire that mars the pattern of horizontals only slants because it is necessary that it go in this direction. In man's complexity and intricacy there is also a beauty, the beauty of functionalism and necessity.

WITH HIS PATTERNS man has often been unkind to nature. But not always. Sometimes in Connecticut he has learned to live with her, become part of her, and even on rare occasions to enhance her. Man's presence is unobtrusive, has to be sought, in this photograph of the Quinnipiac River in the thriving town of North Haven. But man is here. There is a groomed appearance to the river bank that signifies his participation. That looks like a dock or boat of his in the lower left-hand shadows and he may well have planted the willow and other trees along the water's edge. Here he has been nature's friend, with her best interests at heart. In other sections of the river he has erected factories, dumped his waste products into the water. For man is inconsistent and often short-sighted.

MAN AND NATURE are often associates who respect each other, as shown in this photograph taken in Prospect, less than an hour's drive away from urban New Haven. Framed by summer foliage, a typical farm stands as a complete entity. In the foreground cows are in the cowshed; in the background are the large barn, silo, and poultry house. As often, the small white farmhouse seems to indicate it was considered least important in the over-all agricultural establishment. Farming, of course, has decreased in importance with the passing of the years but is still a vital Connecticut occupation. Total income from annual sale of crops is over $58,000,000, and some forty-seven agricultural fairs take place yearly. But it is also true that suburban housing developments have begun to creep into rural towns. However, it will be many years, if ever, before the state's many farmlands vanish. In the meantime the majority of Nutmeg farmers will go on using the land wisely and well.

MAN'S IMPACT UPON NATURE can be small, much, or nothing. He has done nothing to alter this view of Long Island Sound from East Haven beach. It is a place and time when man, for the moment, simply does not exist. Perhaps he is here, in the foreground, beyond the camera's range, watching the cloud-shielded sun gild the waters and hearing the white-spumed waves fall upon the cold rocks. Overwhelmed by his own insignificance, before the majesty of the sea, he may be the millionth man asking the biblical question, "What is Man, that Thou art mindful of him?" But there is no evidence of him in this picture which cannot be dated, not within thousands of years.

TO THE VARIED, well-watered terrain of Connecticut man has brought his structures, beginning with farm buildings and moving on to the factories and plants that have made this a state where manufacturing is the great occupation and a highly skilled labor force an important asset. Besides the major waterway, the Connecticut River, four other rivers, augmented by their tributaries, make their way to the sea. On the banks of one of the latter, the Willimantic, the American Thread Company in 1867 located this factory, now called its "No. 1 Mill." There are thirty-four buildings in the over-all plant now, and water is as important to the firm as it ever was. The river is used for both power and processing materials. Three waterwheels and three steam-driven turbines rely on the resources of the Willimantic. The firm employs about 1,900, has factories in the South as well, and is probably the largest concern in the country manufacturing cotton and synthetic sewing thread, and knitting yarns.

BY CONTRAST with the mill built almost one hundred years ago, here is another "river factory," an important reason why Connecticut is one of the greatest manufacturing states. Sikorsky Aircraft, one of several huge installations in the state operated by United Aircraft, is located on the Housatonic River in Stratford near the Merritt Parkway (visible in foreground). Sikorsky is the world's largest helicopter manufacturer. The plant was opened in 1955 and an engineering wing added in 1958. There are 1,370,000 square feet of manufacturing space on a 250-acre tract which has parking facilities for 4,000 automobiles. The firm employs 8,000 workers. Although Sikorsky does not use the nearby river as a source of power, as earlier factories did, the water does not go to waste. Amphibious helicopters are tested on the Housatonic.

CONNECTICUT'S FIVE MAJOR RIVERS, running to the sea, have mostly helped but sometimes hindered Nutmeggers since the days of the first settlers. North-south traffic could ride on or beside them with ease, but east-west traffic required ferries and bridges. Most of the ferries have vanished but the bridges have grown larger and more important. Here is how man has solved the problem of the Thames River at its mouth between New London and Groton. Piers are available for boats but the Gold Star Memorial Bridge handles all vehicular traffic with modern efficiency and speed. In the background the New Haven Railroad span carries shoreline trains between New York and Boston on one of the country's most scenic routes. Most of the state's rivers have Indian names but not the Thames, although its tributaries, the Willimantic, the Natchaug, the Shetucket and the Quinebaug, all do. The Thames was named for England's most famous river and flows—where else?—past New London to the sea. All industry and farming in Eastern Connecticut have been linked traditionally to this waterway which splits the state from north to south.

IN ADDITION TO STRUCTURES to give him shelter and enable him to move about, man built places to work in. This photograph depicts one of his most impressive in Connecticut. It shows the central portion of the largest Colonial type building in the world—the Aetna Life Insurance Company in Hartford. Connecticut Yankees have always been shrewd businessmen, and in the last decade of the eighteenth century they banded together to insure their merchant ships. Hartford Fire Insurance Co. was founded in 1810, Aetna nine years later, and Hartford became the insurance capital of the United States. The Connecticut insurance companies have total premium and annuity income of $4,158,000,000 per year and total assets of over $16,000,000,000. Aetna itself has assets of $5,120,000,000 and premium income of $1,294,574,000 annually.

CONNECTICUT'S STRUCTURES to house government offices cover a wide range from simple, white, wooden to modern brick and stone buildings. The town hall is the most important edifice in the community but often it will not contain a quorum for a town meeting, which ends up in the firehouse or high school auditorium. Other towns are more fortunate—like Simsbury. A resident, Antoinette Eno Wood, gave this beautiful building to Simsbury. It was built in 1932 at a cost of $325,000, a considerable sum of money for that Depression year.

MAN'S MEETING PLACES in Connecticut are varied but usually signify an interflow of traffic. At the traditional crossroads he established the village. Customarily, a church, white, Congregational, became the meeting house for those who came from different directions on these roads. This is the village of West Stafford, in the piney hills of northeastern Connecticut. It is part of the town of Stafford, established 1719, area 59.4 square miles, population 7,476. Some of the residents of this hamlet can trace their ancestry back to the first settlers. Nothing much goes on here except life, rock-solid, established, and permanent.

AMONG THE MANY EVIDENCES of man in Connecticut none is so revealing as his fences and walls. Essays could be written about them, and probably have, for they disclose much about the Connecticut Yankee. When he was a pioneer settler they were his means of staking out a claim to the wilderness. Essentially they tell about his reverence for neatness and order, his practicality, his sense of independence, and the kind of mutual respect and understanding which is based upon a keen appreciation of who owns what. This scene along Route 7 between Kent and Sharon speaks to us like this: "What's on the near side is yours, on the far side mine. Now, if you want to let the weeds grow rampant on your side, that's your business. I'll keep my land free of 'em."

WHEN ROBERT FROST WROTE that perceptive bit about good fences making good neighbors he probably had something like this in mind, although, to be sure, it is mostly a wall. For this scene in Middlefield near Durham presents the situation nicely—fences and walls in Connecticut have little relationship to those in concentration camps. They are not formidable barriers designed to keep people from moving from one sector to another—they merely mark off property lines and keep livestock from straying. How easy for a neighbor to scramble over this wall! And if he doesn't want to make the effort, a gate has been conveniently added for him to open at will. There is regulation, not barricade. We in Connecticut do not operate hermitages but neither do we believe that liberty means the right to run wild.

THE STORY of the New England wall, one of whose countless samples is shown in this Woodbridge winter picture, has been told many times. With it, the first farmer accomplished three objectives: he cleared his field of rocks and with them he established his property lines and kept his livestock from roaming. This, again, reveals an essential New England trait—making the best of it. That he could not plow and plant with the rocks in the way was a harsh reality. He converted this liability into an asset. It was as simple as that, but the prodigious, back-breaking labor involved astounds our bulldozer-blessed generation which now looks upon his handiwork. Have you ever walked through a Connecticut field, come to a stone wall, and wondered: How long has it been here? How long before every vestige is destroyed? If ever.

THEN THERE IS that observation of Robert Frost's about there being something which doesn't like walls and wants to have them down. That "something" has been at work here along this rather ancient stone wall off Route 81 in Clinton. But perhaps it is not an insidious, mysterious force. What we have here is a battle between stone and wood. Maybe these husky trees just grew too big for their britches and began to push the wall around. They can't win. Someday they will topple and disintegrate into the ground. The boulders will still be there.

MAN ALSO USES FENCES to keep himself out of trouble, either as a physical barrier that forcibly stops him short of danger or, as with this simple rail fence at Merimere, Meriden's reservoir at the foot of Meriden Mountain, as a warning signal, with little actual power to prevent trespassing, intended or accidental. This stark picture, taken toward nightfall on a cloudy day, bears strong black outlines against white and resembles a Japanese print. One final note: the *Connecticut State Manual* gives hundreds of interesting facts about the state, such as the number of houses and the total road mileage. But who has the answer to one omitted statistic?—how many miles of fences and walls?

LIFE IN CONNECTICUT has always been confonted by the sea in the 245 miles of shoreline which faces Long Island Sound. Man has not been able to parcel it out in plots and demark it with stone walls and fences but he has made an attempt to stake out his claims to its usage with piles. It is at best a puny effort but it gives man what little sense of security he can achieve in the ocean. His pilings are erected, fulfill their purposes, and when they are no longer needed are usually left to become rotting relics of human activity. Sometimes, as in this scene along the shorefront in West Haven, where a new beach has been formed, their original function as part of a dock or building foundation, or whatever it may have been, has long since been forgotten.

LONG SINCE FORGOTTEN . . . weatherbeaten pillars, which apparently supported a pier at the foot of Dock Road in South Norwalk, give silent testimony that this desolate marshland area was once the site of nautical activity. It was low tide when the photographer came across this quiet scene. Man's machinations have brought these lofty forest trees from a position of verdant grandeur to this ignominious end. *Sic transit gloria.*

PILINGS HAVE SUPPORTED, as they do here at City Point, New Haven, what has always been a thriving Connecticut industry—oysters. The Indians loved them and so does the white man, but with his Yankee ingenuity and sense of business he made an industry out of them. First offshore cultivation of oyster beds began in 1845 and by the turn of the century they had become a prosperous enterprise, centered in New Haven. From this city, west to Greenwich, oysters were removed from the Sound by the tons. Barrels were sent to London for King Edward VII's coronation. Although the bivalves were responsible for an annual income in the million-dollar bracket, and the industry is still important, there have been adverse modern factors that have harmed the trade. Starfish eat young oysters and man's own pollution of the waters, which he can endure more readily than the sensitive shellfish, has posed a threatening problem.

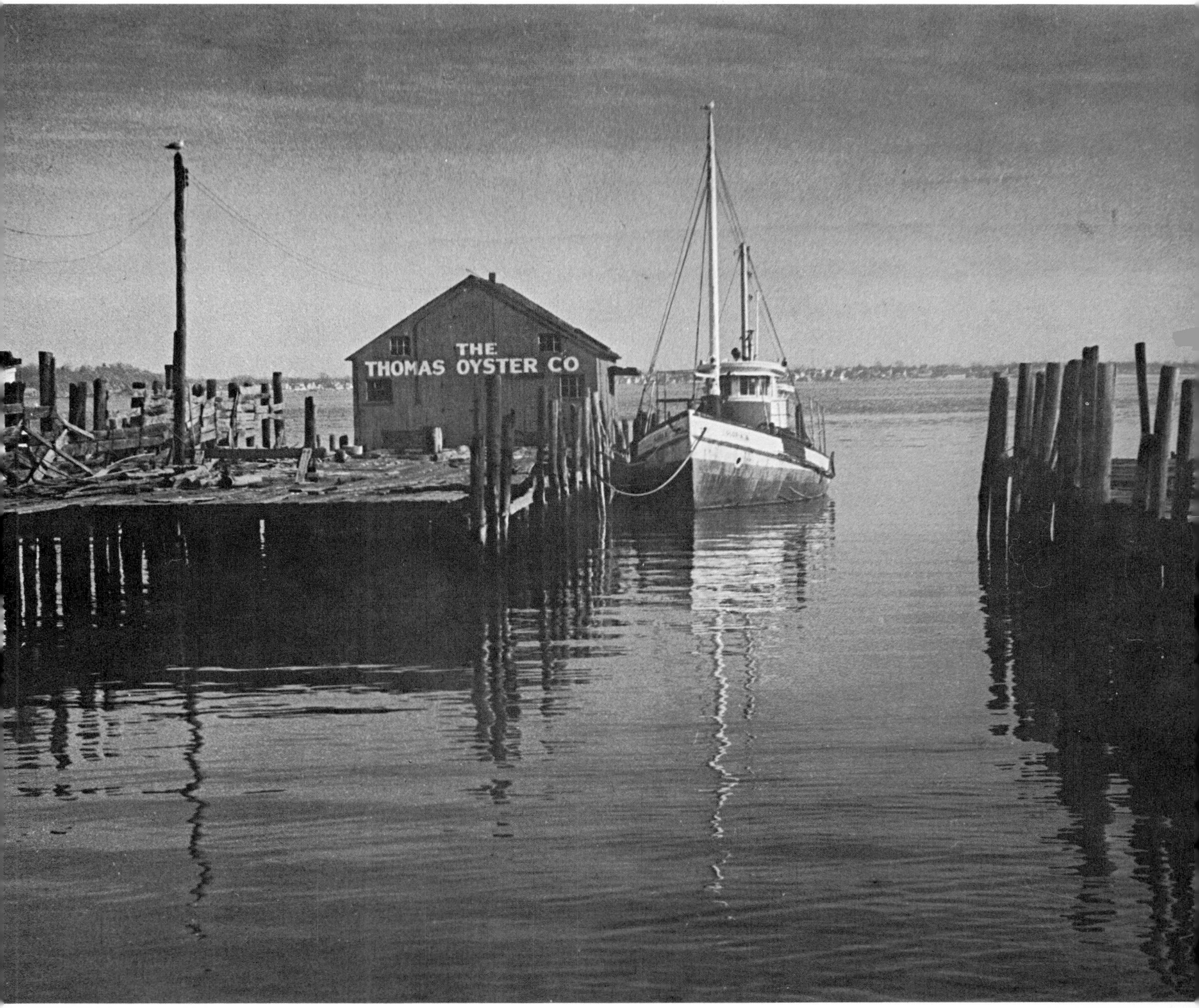
THE
THOMAS OYSTER CO

CAPPED AND CARED-FOR PILINGS indicate a busy waterfront in summertime even though this photograph at Clinton was taken in the middle of winter. Cottages on the distant shore, now boarded up for the season, are noisy with talk and laughter after Memorial Day. But even though winter chases everyone away, she is not a cruel visitor. She has been kinder to this motorboat than its owner and has thoughtfully added a set of white foam rubber cushions to hide its bareness. To the dock and boulders behind it the snow and ice have contributed decorative sheathings and the water glitters coldly under the late afternoon January sun.

BESIDES MARKING OFF THE LAND with fences and walls, and staking feeble claim to the ocean, man has spread travel routes across the state. Nutmeggers have always insisted on good roads, the more the better. The beautifully landscaped Merritt and Wilbur Cross Parkways, the first section of which was opened in 1938, became pioneer models for scenic, well-engineered, no-cross-traffic highways in this country. However, the addition of superhighways did not eliminate other kinds of roads. Today you can find plenty of representatives of the type in this photograph of an old-time country lane which wanders off into farmland here and there in Connecticut. Unimproved and simple, there is one major difference nowadays—passing down it may well be a station wagon instead of a horse. This one is off the Hartford Turnpike between North Haven and Wallingford.

WHEN THE CONNECTICUT vegetable farmer, aware that first to market with the produce gets the top prices, sets out his tomato plants, he may try to jump the gun by a week or so. To do this he uses "hot caps" of translucent paper to protect the younglings from the last few nights of frost that may come. The photographer happened upon this tent city for Lilliputian tomato plants only minutes from the City of New Haven on the old Hartford Turnpike in suburban North Haven. Of course, if you prefer to imagine that an army of little green men with ray guns will come dashing out of these tents——

ANYBODY LOSE A NEEDLE? The haystack represents one of the principal crops of the state, for so long as there are cows and horses that have to be fed, hay must rank high. Other important crops are corn, tobacco, oats, potatoes, apples, peaches, pears, miscellaneous vegetables, and small fruits. There are from 150 to 180 growing days and 50.49 inches of rain a year in Connecticut, and the value of one year's farm income is $58,762,000. As for this picture, taken in Hamburg, a striking proportion has resulted from man's juxtaposition of haystack and pole and hay rake to nature's appletree. Winter has come, there is no room in the barn for hay, and it has settled down from its original pole high position.

IF THE LAST PICTURE had rigid, classic proportions, nature in this one has provided us with a scene of delightful artistic confusion, with corn stalks going every which way. This photo, taken in mid-autumn along the Wallingford Road near Durham with the Blue Hills in the background, glorifies another great Connecticut crop. (Did you ever pick an ear of Connecticut golden bantam corn, drop it immediately into a kettle of boiling water, and soon eat it? Wonderful!) Before the white man ever came to the state the Indian villages were surrounded by cornfields. The settler learned about this vegetable from the Indian and it became his first and most important crop thereafter. In modern times Connecticut agricultural scientists have pioneered in the development of new hybrid strains of corn.

THE CROP that strangers find most difficult to associate with Connecticut is shown in this picture taken in the Windsor area—tobacco. Actually the Indian grew tobacco in small quantities and again the white man learned about it from him. Around 1833 a strain of broadleaf tobacco was introduced and became very popular as wrappers for cigars. At the turn of the century, farmers in the fertile upper Connecticut River Valley introduced the technique of shade-grown tobacco, employing cheesecloth enclosures to simulate a hot, moist tropical climate. Tobacco soon became one of the state's most important crops. After harvesting, the broad leaves are hung to dry in the big sheds shown in the background.

"SNACKTIME! Just a little taste is all we want." Sometimes the assembly-line procedure of moving crops to the barn is interrupted by occasions like this one photographed on a farm at Mt. Carmel. Life would be much tougher all around if a fellow couldn't take ten once in awhile. Didn't you ever hear of the coffee break?

THE COWS HAVE IT GOOD in Connecticut. The air is invigorating, the dairy men up to date, and the scenery is something that a contemplative cud-chewer has time to appreciate. Take this pastoral scene in Shelton. Not like being out on a flat, treeless plain. And when winter comes scudding across the sky and releases the snow, there's a warm barn somewhere in the offing. Anyway, a healthy cow ought to be happy. It's more blessed to give than receive and a cow gives so much of the milk of human kindness.

IN FAIRNESS TO COWS, who have always been regarded as unemotional and rather uncomplicated, we offer this picture of a cow who might have a psychosis. We don't know what her problem is—who can read a cow's mind?—but it looks formidable enough to call in Dr. Joyce Brothers, the eminent female psychologist. Maybe Bossie doesn't like the cameraman. Maybe she's been put on a diet. Or perhaps she wants out from this little pasture so that she can romp with the girls. Or maybe she just doesn't have a satisfactory married life.

YOU CAN'T GO HOME AGAIN. Who says? A cow heads for home whenever it's milking time. Six of them start the long barnward trek at the end of the day as they follow the leader to the milking stool. No. 3 in line turns backward for a moment to chide: "C'mon you kids! The three of you are falling behind." There is a kind of nostalgia about it all. You feel you have been here long ago. Imagine your homesickness if you had not been here for many years and then someone showed you this photo. Perhaps you would remember the lines from Gray's "Elegy":

> The curfew tolls the knell of parting day,
> The lowing herd wind slowly o'er the lea . . .

WATER IS PLENTIFUL in Connecticut, salt and fresh. To draw the latter from its bountiful sources the residents employ a variety of methods from the old-fashioned to the ultramodern. There are plenty of wells in use, although in most cases the pumps are gasoline or electricity driven. Here's a case of the old elbow-grease method being put to use by a little four-year-old girl on a North Guilford farm. She isn't using the old oaken bucket, however, but a contemporary galvanized pail. An old lawn mower (already anything not power-driven seems old!) and a stack of pine firewood attest to the fact that there are chores to be done around this place.

THINK YELLOWSTONE NATIONAL PARK has the only geysers in the U.S.? How about this man-made one, part of a system of water distribution that employs the most modern methods to bring to Connecticut homes and factories the water they need? Thirty-nine cities in the state depend upon reservoirs for their water supply. In this picture of Aspetuck Reservoir in Easton the big fountain is actually the outlet of a tunnel bringing water from the Bridgeport Hydraulic Company's Saugatuck Reservoir two miles away. An estimated twelve million gallons a day flow through the tunnel to the Aspetuck, which in turn empties into the Hemlocks Reservoir, chief source of Bridgeport's water.

SEA-GIRT, RIVER-SPLIT Connecticut has always been anchored to the water as closely as any state can be. By imposing structures upon it man has adapted the water to his own designs, be they practical or esthetic. The former were paramount when he built the Stevenson Dam on the Housatonic River which is pictured here on a bitter cold winter's day from Route 34 on the Oxford side. The dam is 1,213 feet long and has an output capability of 28,750 kilowatts which is utilized by the Connecticut Light & Power Co. Construction of the dam began in the summer of 1917 and the first unit went into operation on November 24, 1919. The pond behind it is approximately ten miles long at crest elevation.

BEAUTY WAS UPPERMOST in his mind when man built the dam which created this photogenic waterfall on Shaffer Road in Bethany near the Woodbridge line. No utilitarian purpose is being served here, but human hands have not worked in vain. They have done well by nature. They have created a scene worth looking at. But it is doubtful that any who worked on the project could have envisioned how lovely it would appear on this sunny February day.

ALWAYS THERE IS the ocean in Connecticut, furnishing work, play, and beauty. And because this is a state of contrasts, the sea and its environs offer many delightful surprises to the imagination. This photograph of sailing boats moored in the Branford River is a good example. When we saw it, it set our imagination to work. We thought of the old days of piracy and smuggling. This suggested to us a smugglers' cove in days of yore with two sailing craft waiting for their crews to return after bringing contraband to consignees in a leafy woodland meeting place. We thought of Longfellow's "Spanish sailors with bearded lips, and the beauty and mystery of the ships." But we had failed to notice something—the television aerial.

IS THE SEA FOR FUN OR FISHING? (And is fishing work or fun?) Anyway, there seems to be a difference of opinion here as to the best uses to which the ocean may be put. Blackie wants to romp. The men are trying to catch shiners at West Haven so that they can go after bigger prey. But their dog seems to be chasing the little fish away. As for that question about fishing being work or fun, it can be both in Connecticut. It is an occupation which gives many a man a livelihood or relaxation that really comes into its own when the blues are running.

THE SEA ALMOST ALWAYS brings out the best in the land. It sand-scours it, washes it, blots out its stains, and points out its weaknesses. It makes land's structures a credit to their surroundings. Witness New London Light, near Ocean Beach Park and diagonally across the Thames River from Groton. This is one of the best-known landmarks on the Connecticut shore and one of the oldest lighthouses in the country. Eighty feet high, it was erected in 1760 and rebuilt in 1801. A new offshore light was installed in 1909. Artists and photographers spend much time at this locale in summertime. Although this is one of the most photogenic lighthouses in the state, the largest is at Stratford Point, at the mouth of the Housatonic River, with a rating of 300,000 candlepower.

CONNECTICUT OFFERS many delightful contrasts in the methods by which its residents and summer visitors take to the waters. You can find just about anything on the waterways, from a kayak to a ferry boat. There has always been canoeing since the arrival of the Indians and although modern man tends to shy away from the sheer motorless labor of paddling, there still is no more satisfying relaxation than a ride in a canoe, especially when you're gliding along at dusk on the Quinnipiac River in Yalesville. Did little brother and his dog horn in on big brother's date? We don't know the exact circumstances here, but having had big brothers with a canoe on a small New England river we know that this is just about tops in boyhood fun. Not all tranquilizers come in small bottles.

NOWADAYS, BOATING is often like this in Connecticut. A cabin cruiser, heading out to sea at Noank, gracefully slides through waters rippled by soft ocean breezes. Our old friends, the pilings, have seen many different kinds of boats pass this point but nothing more sleek or modern. Augmented by an influx of summer visitors, Nutmeggers have taken to the waters in power boats in such numbers that some concern is being expressed for safety factors. It may soon be necessary for pilots to qualify for driving licenses just as motorists do.

YOU CAN SEE a real oldtimer or two in Connecticut if you look around. For instance, the last whaling ship, the *Charles W. Morgan,* is on display at the Mystic Seaport, a museum of the sea. And the vessel shown in the accompanying picture is a three-masted sailing bark, *The Eagle,* used by the Coast Guard Academy on the Thames to train cadets. As part of their schooling to operate the Coast Guard's most modern craft, the cadets learn the ropes of a ship of the past. The experience also steeps them in the lore and tradition of the sea. When *The Eagle* is at berth it may be visited by the public, as may the academy itself.

ONE OF THE PRINCIPAL IMPORTS of Connecticut is petroleum, brought in by big oil tankers such as this. This striking shot, taken from a Sikorsky helicopter, shows a long tanker being berthed in New Haven Harbor by two tugs. In 1961 the import of petroleum products through this port reached a record high—1,620,126,749 gallons. This was an increase of more than one million gallons from the previous year.

IN TANKS LIKE THIS the oil is stored after it has been piped from the tankers entering New Haven Harbor. From this entry port the fuel is shipped into the interior part of the state by tank trucks, perhaps ending up on a farm where the efficient oil burner is a far cry from the old-time wood stoves of another century. Incidentally, it was a New Haven resident, Col. Edwin L. Drake, who first discovered petroleum in Pennsylvania in 1859 and led the way to the replacement of whale oil by kerosene.

THE STATE'S SHORELINE offers us another proof for our paradox which we have been working out in many ways—Connecticut changes but is unchanging. Compare this picture with the one that follows. Here is a traditional scene of the shore, at Guilford. A dock, headquarters of the Thimble Island Oyster Co., a small boat, and piles comprise a picture that looks as if it had always been here for the taking. (Give or take one truck.)

NOW, BY CONTRAST, we are looking at a waterfront scene that is definitely modern and one that would have startled the first oysterboat captains. We are standing at night on the bridge of an oil tanker in New Haven Harbor, gazing at the complex of shipping and industrial installations that makes this an important seaport. Nature seems absent here. Except for the water, all else that can be seen here is man's handiwork. Serving as a distribution point for articles like oil and foreign automobiles, New Haven in a single year handles more than three times as much shipping tonnage as any other state port.

THE WATER OFFERS MORE than boating, be it for business or pleasure, and fishing. It is a bather's paradise. You may think that this photograph shows the cool gorges of the Rockies or an out-of-the-way place in Canada. No, this is Connecticut, where swimming places run the gamut from a huge beach like Hammonasset to your own backyard swimming pool. In between you'll find unusual swimming spots like this one on the Shepaug River at Roxbury Falls. Connecticut has salt-water beaches and shoreline state parks, creeks, rivers, ponds, and lakes of every size and description to swim in. Scarcely anyone in the state lives very far from a body of water of some kind. Some bathers seek out unique places like this one on the Shepaug where there are no crowds; others are more gregarious in their selections. Many of them have a choice of either salt or fresh water swimming not more than an hour or two away, and frequently only a matter of minutes.

SOMETIMES even conventional-looking swimming places can have unusual features. Bathers at Lighthouse Point in New Haven have often paused in their fun to look at these four unique trees in full foliage. Our photographer, however, selected a different time of year so that he could get them in stark silhouette. Like a quartet of slightly mad hags they dance in the ocean wind. They have a right to look weird for they have an unusual story behind them, if legend can be trusted. These are supposed to be persimmon trees, the farthest north any have been found. Lighthouse Point is at the entrance of the harbor and it is said that these trees grew from seeds washed ashore from a wrecked ship. A good photographer just has to like trees and ours is no exception. This, and the following remarkable photographs, show how he caught them in silhouette against the sky and how in so doing he was able to mirror moods that can be translated into human terms.

MEET EUPHROSYNE, Aglaia, and Thalia, the Three Graces, holding forth at Fort Hale Park in New Haven! The classic lines of these three budding willows overlooking Long Island Sound immediately suggested to us the classic trio of the Greeks who were devoted to Grace, Beauty, and Joy.

BY CONTRAST WITH the relaxed beauty, grace, and spring promise of the Fort Hale willows, consider this autumn picture of a pair of willows along the West Haven shore-front. The tanker heading into New Haven Harbor, as if to escape an oncoming storm, and the wind-swept branches of these two trees suggest trouble in the offing. There is beauty here, too, but there are also fear and a sense of fore-boding. A quarter of a century ago your first impression might have been that this was a hurricane brewing off the Gulf Coast. But since 1938 Nutmeggers have been aware that it is almost as likely to be their own coastline. The state has known enough hurricanes to fear annual visitation. Actually the winds here are only thirty miles per hour and the patterns are pleasing, but shoreline residents have learned to be apprehensive in late August and September.

IF NATURE hadn't beaten him to it, the surrealist artist could have imagined this weeping mulberry in New Haven's East Rock Park and had himself a masterpiece. But actually it wasn't all nature's doing. Man created *morus pendula* by grafting shoots upside down on the right-side-up tree. We'll leave it to some disciple of Freud to figure out why anyone would want to make a tree cry. But the result is a fascinating, almost terrifying, creation. If trees were human—and they do weep!—this one might pounce on you should you muster up enough courage to sit under it.

OR TAKE THIS ONE. We call it the "King Lear" Maple because although it once possessed much grandeur, it has suffered misfortune. And yet there is something about its nobility that nothing has been able to destroy completely. You get the idea that this old maple has seen all things, suffered all things, endured all things. One day a bolt of lightning or a hurricane gale took a cruel shot at it and beheaded it to this despairing state. And then the photographer came riding along Barnes Road in Wallingford, saw its possibilities, and gave it new life and meaning.

HERE ARE SILHOUETTES in miniature, both as nature unconsciously created them and as man has unwittingly imitated her work. Like Christmas ornaments on a tree, the buttonballs in one photograph hang from a huge sycamore. These splotched giants are among the most colorful trees in Connecticut and are reported to be the first of the hardwoods to grow on earth. Suggested titles for this offbeat picture: "Black on White," "Circles and Lines," "Sycamore in Silhouette." Its artistry may suggest others to you. But there is more than artistry here. The complete miracle of life hangs pendulously in the balance, hoping for the warm envelopment of the soil from which the parent sycamore came and in which it now stands firmly rooted. The other photo shows how man, quite accidentally, has followed the motif that nature set when he built this system of overhead electric wires for New Haven Railroad trains.

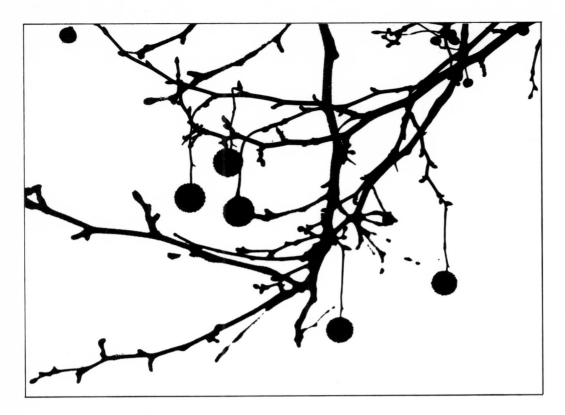

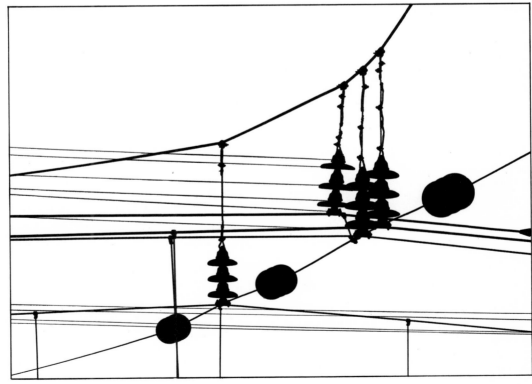

THIS TREE SILHOUETTE will probably puzzle most viewers, even those from Connecticut where it actually represents one of the most common roadside sights—the staghorn sumac. In autumn its leaves turn first and present early evidence of the imminent glory of fall; its foliage is brilliant and offers some compensation for those who complain about the sumac's rank, weed-like growth all summer. In Greenwich the photographer caught an unusual aspect of the sumac—its angular dark stalks suggesting the hairy antlers of a young stag.

A TREE GROWS IN BROOKLYN? No, Connecticut. New Haven, to be exact, only a few miles away from country scenes where trees are unimpeded by man. Between buildings on Orange Street this tree has groped upwards a long, long way to find the sun and a chance to add to its foliage. The shadows indicate the light is strong and worth seeking if one will just make the effort. From darkness and confinement the heavens can yet be sought. We call this picture "Aspiration." It represents a pattern that has been achieved by man and Nature working with, against, or in spite of each other. Take your choice.

HERE THE PATTERNS are all man's. In the Mystic Seaport he has achieved a museum of nineteenth-century New England coastal village life which annually attracts visitors from all parts of the country. At left, beyond the old wagon, may be seen the bow of the last whaling ship to operate, the *Charles W. Morgan.* The various shops throughout the village enable the sightseer to witness how articles were made in the whaling days. To visit Mystic is to step back into another century, one in which Connecticut is proud to have played a leading role in the exciting drama of man vs. sea.

IT MUST BE OBVIOUS after looking at the last photograph, and most of the others in this book, that much of the cameraman's time is spent planning pictures. Sometimes it means waiting for a few hours until sun and shadow are just right. At other times he even waits for seasons to arrive and give him the effects he is seeking. Success for a photographer is a combination of imagination, technical skill, patience, and plain hard work. Oh, yes, we left out something—a little bit of luck. Here the photographer was taking shots for a feature story on a doctor in Derby. He noted a statue of a cat which had been sculpted by the doctor's wife. Suddenly a real cat jumped up for a look at its likeness and curled its tail in the same way as the statue. Larry grabbed the picture fast. Luck is important but you have to be ready to capitalize on it.

AND WHILE WE'RE ON THE SUBJECT of felines, here's another great cat picture Larry took one day in Lyme—a cat scratching itself. Like we say, if you're going to do something, put your heart and soul into it. Put——Pardon us a second while we reach back. It itches right there between the shoulder blades. Ah, that's better!

THINKING ABOUT unusual animal pictures suggested this one and so we hunted it up. Whether you regard them as a colorful addition to the Green or a nuisance doesn't bother New Haven's famous pigeons. These guardians of the Green are on duty every day of the year, regardless of the weather. Here Larry photographed a pair after a snowstorm when their tracks and those of scores of their friends had made a fascinating quilt-work pattern for the camera to record. When you come to New Haven, be sure to feed the pigeons.

FARMERS DON'T FEEL so kindly toward birds, however, as shown on a farm near Stafford Springs. Perhaps this picture is as good as any to demonstrate our thesis that Connecticut has changed, but is unchanging. Scarecrows have been a fixture on the state scene since time immemorial and probably will be until the scientist invents invisible force fields (we read science fiction) to keep the birds away. But today's scarecrows show many evidences of modern civilization. This farmer has used an aluminum foil pie tin and a coffee bag from the co-op store to fashion the head of the fellow in the foreground. The guy in the rear sports an ironworker's helmet!

NATURE IS PERSISTENT and rugged in Connecticut, where unwanted vegetation has learned to combat rocky soil and occasionally harsh winters. Let man relax but a moment and wild growth sneaks in and encroaches upon his cultivated plans. The farmer had better keep careful watch on this cornfield in Orange because weeds, wild grape, and other trespassers have the vitality to take over at a moment's notice.

EVEN IN DEATH Nature can be rugged. This Cedar of Lebanon died in the hurricane of 1938 which struck a brutal blow at the Connecticut coast. But a Yale professor, George Izenour, who has a home on Governor's Island in the Thimble Islands, was so impressed by its symmetry and beauty that he decided it should be preserved. He encased its roots in cement and it still "lives" on, a striking attraction of the summer shoreline.

YANKEE VITALITY derives much from Nature's quiet demonstration that, regardless of the circumstances, life must go on—in fact, draw sustenance from death. Here, in the forest on Bethany Mountain, Nature is lavish with evidences of growth and decay. Dead trees stretch along the ground which will eventually absorb them and use them to promote new life. Dying branches jut from older trees and soon will slip earthward. But, beyond, the sun is shining in the woodland and new leafy growth heads skyward.

LIFE FEEDS ON DEATH, clinging precariously to any toehold. In Wilton a dying birch is host to an assortment of fungus invaders which project shelflike from the bark and carry on an existence which seems to be of importance only to themselves.

FRESH FALL FLOWERS bloom from the decadent environment of a West Redding forest oak which will not be standing much longer. Whether this is a sad or happy scene depends on where your sympathies lie—with oak or blossom. But the flowers prove two points: Life should not be afraid of death, and Nature has room for many forms and specimens in various stages of ascent or decline.

AMONG NATURE'S FORMS there is infinite variety. One of these, just plain old Connecticut swamp grass, grows unchecked, although civilization is close to this marsh near the manufacturing city of Stamford. It is not difficult to find a scene like this close to any urban center in the state. The backyard of busy, bustling, industry-minded Connecticut is Nature, accessible and always present.

DRAWING BACK FROM the closeup of swamp grass, we find an entrancing vista of a tidal flat which the state hopes to preserve through a conservation program like this one in Stony Creek. From the earliest times Nutmeg State residents have found peace and solace in the quiet contemplation of such idyllic scenes. They're good for the soul.

OUR EXPLORATION into the many aspects of Connecticut life, past and present, had to lead us to this picture sooner or later. To many, regardless of religion, this photograph may be the most easily recognized symbol of Connecticut that exists—the old white Congregational Church which has been so much a part of the state's history and which has been exported elsewhere throughout the United States, notably to Ohio. There are many other religions in Connecticut now, and churches of different architectures, but still the old village church with tall white spire, beckons its faithful for miles around in communities throughout the state. The Hampton Church, organized in 1723, is the second oldest Congregational Church building in the state. It has an overhang, supported by Doric columns and its steeple features rectangular construction. Congregationalism, still the leading Protestant sect in numbers (latest figures show there are 304 churches, 501 ministers and 141,021 members) was once the established church of Connecticut. It was disestablished in 1818.

OUTLINED AGAINST THE SKY above the trees, the slim spire of the First Church of Christ Congregational is a familiar Farmington landmark. Built in 1771, it is considered one of New England's most beautiful traditional churches. From its pulpit, and from many others in the state, came ardent sermons against British oppression at the time of the Revolution. The church is still vigorous. W. Storrs Lee, who has put his finger on the Connecticut pulse expertly in *Yankees of Connecticut,* has commented: "In northern New England many a Protestant church stands neglected and abandoned on a deserted hilltop, but few of the Connecticut meeting-houses have suffered this indignity. As rural communities expanded into suburban and rural-urban centers, the old churches have seen a corresponding growth. Most of the original Congregational church doors are still open on Sunday morning. The sermons are shorter, the doctrine less platitudinous, the music more melodious, but the basic faith of the Connecticut fathers lives on, refined and revitalized."

ONE OF THE MOST PHOTOGRAPHED CHURCHES in Connecticut is the lovely Madison Congregational, set back from the town green. This is the third structure on the site. The first was erected in 1705, a plain, barnlike building with no paint or adornment of any kind. The congregation was called to worship by drum, and men and women sat on opposite sides of the aisle. The minister was the Reverend John Hart, the first regular graduate of Yale. A second, larger meetinghouse was built in 1743 and was so cold and uncomfortable that churchgoers put up "Sabbath Day houses" on the Green so that they could warm up before and between the two-hour services. Eventually stoves were installed in the church. The present building was completed in 1838, its construction marred when two workmen were killed by one of the beams. Today the church could not hold all the camera fans who have taken its picture.

THIS TRANSPLANTED LITTLE CHURCH is one of the most interesting and picturesque in the state. For seventy years it had stood in Fishtown, near New London, for the spiritual solace of fishermen and others who take to the sea or are left behind. In 1949 it was moved to Mystic to become part of the Mystic Seaport, the reconstructed New England coastal village which has become one of Connecticut's greatest tourist attractions. While visiting the port many stop in at Fishtown Chapel to say a prayer. Mystic, which has been called "the living museum of the sea," contains about twenty acres of re-created nineteenth-century New England, with craft shops, planetarium, and a valuable whaling collection, including the last whaling ship *Charles W. Morgan,* the training ship *Joseph Conrad,* and another ship, the *Bowdoin,* all of which can be boarded by visitors.

THE NEW EXISTS SIDE BY SIDE with the old in Connecticut. This has been one of the persistent themes running through our book and nowhere does it receive more impressive confirmation than with churches. Remembering the churches you have just been viewing, look at this and the next two pictures. This is St. Mark's Evangelic Church in Norwich, an excellent example of modern architecture, although rather "far out" from traditional Colonial or Gothic designs. While the old and traditional remains in Connecticut, the new and streamlined comes in. And, surprisingly, there is little friction. Some like the old, some the new, but most agree both are beautiful. An editor has commented: "The recent trend toward modern church buildings has created truly beautiful additions to the Connecticut landscape." The word additions is the important one; nothing has been taken away.

CONNECTICUT HAD FEW JEWS in Colonial times, although in legislative papers there is mention of a "David the Jew" as early as 1659. In 1818, with the disestablishment of the Congregational Church, other Christians were first guaranteed religious freedom. When in 1843 this right was extended to non-Christians, German Jews migrated in great numbers to the state. In the 1880's Jews from Eastern Europe began to pour in. Now the most recent statistics show the state having 101,300 Jews, 80 synagogues and 70 rabbis. In recent years Jewish congregations have been responsible for building many strikingly modern and beautiful synagogues like the one shown here—Congregation B'nai Israel on Bridgeport's Park Avenue.

FROM THEIR ORIGINAL STATUS as a minority which was subjected to hostility and some persecution, Roman Catholics have increased in numbers through the years to become the dominant religion in Connecticut, especially in the cities. Although their numbers were small before the nineteenth century, they increased greatly in the latter part of the century, their biggest jump being in the 1890-1906 imigration wave when they climbed from 152,945 to 352,368. Today there are estimated to be 1,159,757 Catholics, 330 parishes and 1,312 priests in the state. Connecticut Catholics have also shown a preference for modern religious architecture. When their huge brownstone cathedral, St. Joseph's, burned in 1956, they raised money to build the superb cathedral in Hartford, shown here, at a cost of $10,000,000. Formal opening ceremonies were held in May, 1962. But although the contemporary design shows the modern trend, Catholics, like other Connecticut churchgoers, did not desert the past. Many relics, rescued from the fire of the old cathedral, were installed in the new.

CHURCHES HAVE ALWAYS BEEN in the midst of life in Connecticut, the very heart and soul of the community. Much of the activity that goes on in the small towns centers around the village church and in the larger cities parish units are the important factor. It is difficult—nay, impossible—to be a photographer in Connecticut and not have churches crop up consistently in your pictures, even when they are not the focal point of interest. These cows proceed across the highway near the Episcopal Church at Quaker Farms, part of Oxford, knowing they have the right of way and taking their own sweet time about exercising it. Cars sometimes clog the curbs in Connecticut but cows can still be found meandering across the roads as they have for centuries, even though the stuff underfoot be macadam now and not dirt.

LIFE IN ALL ITS STAGES, all its ages, has passed by, around, and through the New Haven Green and its three churches (here you can see the middle one, Center Congregational) during the centuries. Here have walked the high and the mighty, presidents, governors, mayors, Yale students of generation after generation, throngs of citizens, the poor and the wealthy, and the halfway in between. And some of them, when the weather was fine, have just sat down, talked, waited for a bus, or read the newspaper. Among them is this popcorn vendor who has done a lot of business at this spot in his time, who does not specialize in the hard sell and who is not about to get himself a case of ulcers like a Madison Avenue executive. Life's too short— and sweet.

BUT IN THE MIDST OF LIFE we are in death. Another paradox. And the last one—that in this densely populated, energetic and vital state this must be so. Hallowed tombs of the patriots. Venerated burying grounds like New Haven's Grove Street. Age-old crypts. Modern crematories. Newly opened cemeteries. And long-neglected ones like this one in Easton, giving us our final Connecticut contrast—that nature has remembered where man has forgotten and with the kindness of her black-eyed Susans and Queen Anne's lace has seen fit to decorate the graves of these, our forefathers.

BUT WE DON'T WANT TO END our book with the finality of death. The state's past has been glorious but its present is exciting. And the future holds promise. As it did in our very first photograph, a pleasant road again lies invitingly open ahead of us. Here, near Torrington, it seems to be only slightly traveled, but as the eye moves on into the woods the prospect is appealing. One feels that if the foot could follow the eye the end result would be a happy one. This is the way it usually is in "Pictorial Connecticut."